# ROADSIDE
# *Wild Flowers*
## OF CHRISTIAN COUNTY

# ROADSIDE
# Wild Flowers
## OF CHRISTIAN COUNTY

## Sue Robinson

Oak Tree Press                    Taylorville, IL

# Oak Tree Press

Oak Tree Books may be purchased for educational, business, or sales promotional use. Contact Publisher for quantity discounts.

Printed in Shanghai, China by Sunquest, Inc.

First Edition, June 2007

10 9 8 7 6 5 4 3 2 1

Cover and Interior Design by Mick Andreano, http://www.mickadesign.com/

Although some wildflowers are edible, there are many poisonous species, and it may be difficult to distinguish between them. Do not eat any plant you find growning wild.

Library of Congress Cataloging-in-Publication Data

Robinson, Sue, 1946 --
   Roadside wildflowers of Christian county / by Sue Robinson.
      p. cm.
   ISBN 978-1-892343-43-7 (alk. paper)
1. Wild flowers--Illinois--Christian County--Identification. 2. Wild flowers--Illinois--Christian County--Pictorial works. I. Title.
   QK157.R63 2007
   582.1309773'81--dc22
                        2007001814

*I* would like to thank my husband, Bruce Robinson, for his patience throughout this project and especially for the many times he willingly pulled off the road so I could collect a new plant. I wish also to thank Gary Letterly of the University of Illinois Cooperative Extension Service for his encouragement and also his help in identifying various blossoms. Finally, I would like to give credit to my father, Tom Kirkpatrick, for passing on his love and knowledge of plants and nature.

*I* would like to dedicate this book in memory of Lee J. Robinson (1977 - 2006) who loved the outdoors from the golf courses to the ski slopes.

*T*he purpose of this book is to help people enjoy the satisfaction of identifying and naming the roadside flowers, which they drive by everyday. Since all of the flowers in this book can be seen from the road, everyone can use it, not just those who are able to hike the woods and trails. As people become familiar with the local wildflowers and appreciate their beauty, I hope they will then work to preserve and protect them.

The idea for this book first came about when I began to identify the flowers I saw on my daily jogging route. I was surprised at how many different species there were in just a few square miles. I then started painting each flower, often more than once in order to get it just right. Over ten years, I accumulated a collection of 64 paintings. In order to share these with other interested people, I decided to put them into a book. For ease of identification, I have organized them by color. I have also included a map of Christian County with the location of each flower painted marked with a number.

This quotation by Louis Pasteur sums up my feelings. "The more I study nature, the more I stand amazed at the work of the Creator."

## Parts of a Flower

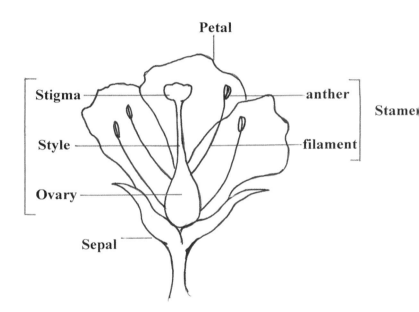

# Leaf Types

**Lance-shaped**

**Oval**

**Palmate**

**Toothed**

**Lobed**

## PENNYCRESS - *Thlaspi arvense*

| April - Aug. | Grows from 6 to 8 inches. |
| --- | --- |

Pennycress gets its name from the flat, notched seed pods that turn reddish brown as they mature and resemble pennies. It is a shallow rooted annual that grows in fields, pastures, lawns, and roadsides. As a member of the mustard family the tiny flowers have 4 white petals. The blossoms grow in loose clusters atop the stems. The leaves are alternate and clasp the stem with earlike projections. When eaten by dairy cows they impart a bitter flavor and odor to the milk.

## STRAWBERRY, WILD - *Fragaria virginiana*

| April - May. | Grows from 3 - 8 inches. |
|---|---|

Wild strawberry flowers have 5 white petals and many stamens like most members of the rose family. The name comes from the words streaw berige, because it spreads by strewing its runners in all directions. The small red berries are among the sweetest of all prairie fruits, delicious for eating fresh or making into preserves. Larger commercial hybrids are not as sweet. Issac Walton is credited with saying, " Doubtless God could have made a better berry, but doubtless God did not. "

## FLEABANE, DAISY - *Erigeron strigosus*

| April - August. | Grows from 1 to 3 feet. |
|---|---|

The flowers of Daisy Fleabane are from 1/2 to 1 inch across. They are made up of 50 - 100 white rays around a yellow disk and are slightly fragrant. The leaves are hairy and elliptical on long stems. This widespread annual is a member of the sunflower family. Dried bunches were said to repel fleas. White tailed deer browse on this species.

| BLACKBERRY - *Rubus allegheniensis* | |
| --- | --- |
| May - June. | Arching branches up to 7 ft long. |

The blackberry leaves consist of 3-5 toothed leaflets. The recurved thorns are sharp and strong. The flowers which grow in clusters all along the stems are made up of five petals around a star shaped center. The juicy black fruit appears in July with some of the berries as large as 1 1/2 inches. It is a member of the Rose family.

SKR
5/02

| DOGBANE (INDIAN HEMP) - *Apocynum cannabinum* | |
|---|---|
| May - Aug. | Grows to 3 feet. |

Dogbane has clusters of tiny bell shaped blossoms, white or greenish white and red stalks. The oval shaped, blue green leaves are opposite with definite stems. It is closely related to milkweed. Early Indians used the fibers from the stalks to make cords for fishing lines, baskets, and mats. When bruised all part of the plant exude a white sap, which is slightly poisonous.

SKR 7/05

## POKEWEED - *Phytolacca americana L.*

| May - Oct. | Grows to 10 feet. |
|---|---|

This plant is a Native American. It has racemes of little white flowers followed by dark purple juicy berries on smooth red stems. The name comes from the Indian word, Pokan, meaning red juiced plant. It was used as a stain or dye by the Indians and early settlers. In 1845, twigs of this plant were worn by followers of James Polk for president. The early leaves may be eaten in a salad but the mature plant is considered poisonous.

SYR

| QUEEN ANNE'S LACE (WILD CARROT) - *Daucus carota.* | |
|---|---|
| May - Oct. | Grows from 1-4 feet. |

This many branched plant has compound umbrels made up of tiny 5 petaled blossoms. Legend has it that the young Queen Anne pricked her finger while making lace, causing a drop of blood to fall on the lace. That is why in the very center of each creamy-white umbrel is a tiny blossom of deepest red. As the flower withers, the umbrel folds up forming a bird's nest shape into which the seeds fall.

SKR
4/06

| HORSE NETTLE - *Solanum carolinense* | |
|---|---|
| May - Oct. | Grows from 6 - 18 inches. |

These flowers grow in clusters at the end of the stems. The 5 white, changing to purple, petals are joined to form a star shape. The bright yellow stamens protrude from the center. The spiny leaves are favored by the potato beetle. This plant produces smooth yellow berries that look like small tomatoes but are not considered edible. In spite of its name, the only animal with a tough enough mouth to eat this prickly plant is the sheep.

Horse Nettle

SKR
6/00

| YARROW, MILFOIL - Achillea millefolium | |
|---|---|
| May - Nov. | Grows from 2 -2 1/2 feet. |

The stiff stems of Yarrow have many very finely divided, fernlike leaves. The flowers grow at the top of each stem in a flat cluster. The tiny petals are white with a yellow center. The entire plant is aromatic and when eaten by cows, gives the milk an unpleasant flavor. It is also repellant to insects. In Greek legend, Achilles used yarrow leaves as medicine during the plague. European Gypsies called it carpenter's herb since it was used to staunch bleeding wounds, a hazard of this occupation.

SKR 12/01

## WHITE CAMPION- *Lychnis alba*

| June-Aug. | Grows from 1 1/2 - 2 1/2 feet. |
| --- | --- |

The stems of the Campion plant are branched, hairy, and sticky. The flowers are about 3/4 inch across and have five petals each one deeply cleft. They have an inflated calyx, which is finely veined in red. The leaves are long and pointed and grow opposite. They open in late afternoon or evening. The male and female flowers grow on separate plants and the male has a smaller calyx.

White
Campion

SKR
5/03

## HEDGE PARSLEY - *Torilis arvensis*

| June - August. | Grows to 2 1/2 feet. |
|---|---|

This plant has many branches with flat-topped umbels growing above the foliage. The white flowers are quite small on long stems. The leaves are alternate, narrow, and pinnately divided. The fruit is small, round and bristly, sticking to clothes and fur. Hedge parsley is an annual and a native of Europe.

Hedge parsley    SKR 7/05

## POISON HEMLOCK - *Conium maculatum*

| June - Aug. | Grows from 2 to 6 feet. |
|---|---|

This plant is a biennial, which forms a rosette the first year. It is a member of the carrot family, but all parts of the plant are very poisonous. The stems are smooth and hollow and have purple splotches on them. The tiny, white flowers are in flat topped clusters. The leaves are finely divided and toothed with a lacy appearance. It is believed that Poison Hemlock was used in the death of Socrates.

## TEASEL- *Dipsacus fullonum*

| June - Oct. | Grows to 8 feet. |
|---|---|

Teasel has a straight, branched and prickly stem, which supports the large cylindrical head. On this head, the small pale lilac or cream colored flowers bloom in a ring. Stiff bracts taller than the head extend upwards. The upper leaves are joined around the stem. The dried heads were used for combing hair by Indians and early pioneers and later to tease the nap up on woolen cloth.

SKR 7/05

## ONION, WILD - *Allium canadense*

| July - Aug. | Grows from 1 -2 feet. |
|---|---|

A member of the onion or garlic family, this plant has a strong smell. It is good for flavoring soups and stews, and the early explorers learned from the Indians that it would help prevent scurvy. The flowers are tiny with 3 pale pink petals and 3 petal-like sepals. Among these sterile flowers, form top setting bulbils or bulbets which will grow into new plants.

SKR 6/05

## ASTER, FROST - *Aster pilosus*

| Sept - Oct. | Grows up to 4 feet. |
|---|---|

Frost Aster blossoms have many white florets around a yellow center, which turns red after pollination. The flowers are small, only 3/4 inch across. They bloom on secondary stems from curving main stems. There are hundreds of varieties. This perennial is one of the most common. Aster is the Greek word for star, and is found in many words such as astronomy, astrology, and asterisk (small star). Pilosus means with soft hair.

## CRESSLEAFED GROUNDSEL (GOLDEN RAGWORT, BUTTERWEED) -
*Senecio glabellus*

| May - July. | Grows to 2 1/2 feet. |
|---|---|

This flower has small yellow blossoms clustered at the top of ribbed stems. Each blossom has between 12 - 21 rays. They turn into downy seed heads when ripe. It has the raggedy leaves of the ragwort family but the basal leaves are egg shaped. It is a common weed in no-till or reduced tillage fields. It is poisonous to livestock and humans.

SKR
5/99

## CINQUEFOIL, ROUGH FRUITED - *Potenilla recta*

| April - June. | Grows from 2-2 1/2 feet. |
|---|---|

This perennial is a member of the Rose family. The name is French for five leaves. There are usually 5 but sometimes 7 leaves divided palmately. Many cinquefoils are native though some species are from Europe. The flowers have 5 heart shaped, pale yellow petals on stiff, bushy stems. Each flower lasts one day. They sometimes grow in large colonies and are shunned by grazing animals.

6/03
SKR

Rough-fruited
Cinquefoil

## YELLOW ROCKET - *Barbarea vulgaris*

| April - June. | Grows to 2 feet. |
|---|---|

Yellow Rocket is a much branched plant of the mustard family. The leaves are primarily in a basal rosette. The small crowded yellow flowers are in terminal bunches. They have 4 petals arranged in a cross shape. The flowers are self-fertile and are pollinated by flies, bees, and beetles. The long slender seedpods, about one inch long, form along the stems as the flowering continues.

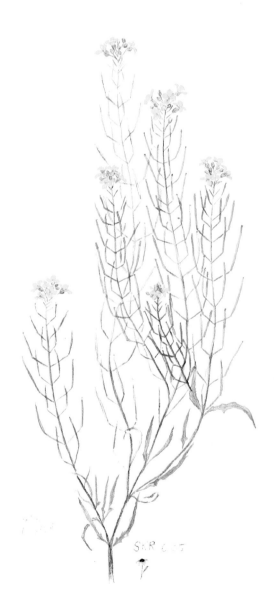

## DANDELION *-Taraxacum officinale*

| March - Sept. | Grows from 3-10 inches. |
|---|---|

Dandelions are one of earliest signs of spring. They have a long tap-root making them difficult to eradicate. They have hollow stalks, which produce a milky sap. The yellow blossom are 1-2 inches across and stay low until the seed head is ripe when it then puts on a growth spurt rising above the grass line, allowing the wind to catch and disperse the seeds. The early spring leaves can be eaten as salad or boiled as greens while the blossoms can be made into wine or tonic. The name comes from the French "dente de lion" meaning tooth of the lion referring to the jagged edges of the leaves which grow in a low basal rosette. It originally came from Europe.

## YELLOW SALSIFY (YELLOW GOATSBEARD) - *Tragopogon dubius*

| May - July. | Grows from 1 - 3 feet. |
|---|---|

The fleshy stalks of Salsify are topped by light yellow, medium-sized flowers whose narrow bracts extend past the petals. The flowers close by noon on sunny days when the plant then resembles a candleabrum. The leaves are grass-like and sometimes have a blue-green tint. The seed head is a large attractive puffball.

SKR
2/05

## SAINT JOHN'S WORT - *Hypericum perforatum*

| May - Sept. | Grows from 1-3 feet. |
|---|---|

St. John's Wort is a shrub-like plant with many branches. The 1/2 inch flowers grow in clusters. They have five yellow petals sometimes with small black dots on the edges. It got its name because it comes into bloom around June 24, the feast day of St. John the Baptist. There are dozens of native species, and several imports. It is sometimes regarded as soothing to the nerves. In medieval times it was hung over the doorway to ward off lightning, fire, and witches.

St. John's Wort

| BUTTER AND EGGS (TOADFLAX) - *Linaria vulgaris* | |
| --- | --- |
| May-Sept. | Grows from 1-3 feet. |

Butter and Eggs will grow anywhere and can become a nuisance. Similar to a snapdragon, it was imported for gardens, but soon escaped. Each flower has pale yellow upper petals and a bright orange lower lip. No insect can enter unless heavy enough to force open the lower petal to reach the long nectar spur. The story is told of a little yellow dragon who died when a fried egg (always death to dragons) became stuck in his throat and he was then transformed into the butter and eggs flower.

Butter
&
Eggs

SKR
7/00

| BLACK-EYED SUSAN - *Rudbeckia hirta* | |
|---|---|
| May - Oct. | Grows to 2 1/2 feet. |

Along the roadsides and meadows, Black-eyed Susans brighten the view. The rich yellow petals surround the deep purple-brown centers, creating an attractive flower. Many people have transplanted these flowers to their own gardens where they usually reseed themselves for years. The leaves and stems are very downy which keeps the summer dust from clogging the breathing pores (stomata).

SKR
7/00

Black-eyed
Susan

## MULLEIN, GREAT - *Verbascum thapsus*

| May - Sept. | Grows from 1 to 7 feet. |
|---|---|

This biennial has a rosette of downy grayish green leaves the first year, and then the second year a tall stem topped by a spike covered with small, yellow, tubular flowers. The open flowers are scattered randomly about the spike. It has been called the Saugero of the prairie as it towers over the landscape. Mullein is from the Latin mollis meaning soft. The early settlers learned from Indians to line their babies' diapers with the soft leaves. The dried stalks were sometimes dipped in tallow and used for torches.

[Great Mullein]

SKR
7/96

## PARSNIP, WILD - *Pastinaca sativa*

| May - Oct. | Grows from 2 - 5 feet. |
|---|---|

The stout grooved stem of Wild Parsnip supports flat umbrels of small yellow flowers. Each umbrel is placed horizontally to receive full sun. The leaf stems clasp the stalk. The leaves are long, compound with 5 to 15 leaflets, and bright green. The sap can cause severe blistering of the skin. It is a native of Europe.

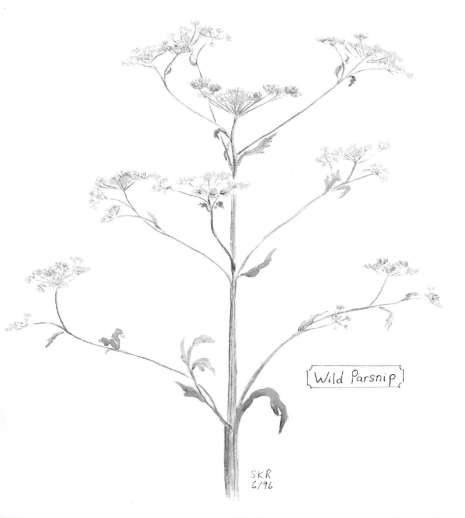

Wild Parsnip

SKR
6/96

## BIRD'S-FOOT TREFOIL - *Lotus corniculatus*

| June - Sept. | Grows from 6 - 12 inches. |
|---|---|

This low growing member of the Pea family thrives in dry rocky soil. It is a short lived perennial usually living from 2 - 4 years. The leaves are divided into 5 leaflets. The flowers are bright yellow, 3/4 in long, and popular with butterflies. The seedpod looks like a bird's foot. It is a native of Europe that was once used for blue and yellow dye.

Birdsfoot
Trefoil

SKA

## MULLEIN, MOTH - *Verbascum blattaria*

| June - Sept. | Grows from 2 - 3 feet. |
|---|---|

Moth Mullein spikes have several one inch blossoms open at a time. Each flower has 5 round, white or yellow petals that are deep red at the center. There are also 5 red fuzzy stamens that look like the antenna of a moth. Moth Mullein is a biennial, forming a basal rosette of leaves the first year and then flowering spikes with alternate leaves the second year. It is a member of the snapdragon family and not a native of North America.

Moth
Mullein

SKR
5/00

## EVENING PRIMROSE - *Oenothera biennis*

| June - Oct. | Grows from 2-5 feet. |
| --- | --- |

The light yellow flowers of Evening Primrose have 4 petals with 4 bent back sepals forming a tube. The large pistil is in the shape of an X. The flowers open in late afternoon and are pollinated by night-flying insects. The narrow, lance-shaped leaves have a silvery sheen as they are covered by many short hairs. It is tolerant of most soil types. Some larger flowered varieties are grown commercially for their oil.

Evening Primrose

SKR
8/97

## FLOWER OF AN HOUR (VENICE MALLOW) -
### Hibiscus trionum

| July - Sept. | Grows 1-2 feet. |
|---|---|

Each pale yellow blossom with a dark magenta center remains open only a few hours, which is how it was named Flower of an Hour. The sepals then close to form the translucent husks. The leaves are very irregular. The mallow family is named from the Greek word meaning soft because of the soothing gelatinous texture of the roots.

SKR 6/05

## DOCK, PRAIRIE - *Silphium terebinthinaceum*

| July- Aug. | Grows from 4-10 feet. |
|---|---|

The resin in the leaves and stems of Prairie Dock has the odor of turpentine, hence the Latin name. In spring the plant produces large, spade shaped basal leaves covered with a rough waxy layer which reduces evaporation. Then, in August, smooth red stalks grow up quite tall with round buds that open into small yellow sunflowers.

## PARTRIDGE PEA - *Chamaecrista fasciculata*

| July - Sept. | Grows to 2 feet. |
|---|---|

The flowers of Partridge Pea have 5 bright yellow asymmetrical petals with a spot of purple at each base. The stamen are flared to one side. The blossoms grow from the leaf axils and are about 1 inch across. The seeds are eaten by ground dwelling birds. The leaflets may even be sensitive to the touch and fold up when handled, and they also may fold up during the heat of the day.

## COMPASS-PLANT - *Silphium laciniatum*

| July-Sept. | Grows from 5 -8 feet. |
|---|---|

The stout densely hairy stem of the Compass-Plant is tough and resinous. The bright yellow flowers are 2-3 inches across and occur alternately, spirally. The leaves are deeply lobed and often put their edges North to South leaving the broad part facing the sun, East and West, hence the name Compass-plant. This is a native prairie plant whose sticky sap was sometimes used by Native Americans as a chewing gum.

SKR
1/06

## SOWTHISTLE, SPINY - *Sonchus arvensis*

| July - Oct. | Grows from 1 1/2 - 5 feet. |
| --- | --- |

This plant has spiny leaves whose heart shaped bases clasp the stem while the rest of the leaf curves strongly back. The flowers are a bright yellow and turn into small puffballs when ripe. It is not a true thistle. It is native to Europe and Asia where it got its common name from being fed to sows. It is deep rooted and can colonize rapidly, depleting the nitrogen in the soil.

Spiny Sowthistle

SKR
7/98

## SUNFLOWER, COMMON - *Helianthus annuus*

| July - Nov. | Grows to 10 feet. |
|---|---|

Sunflower's stout hairy stems support large oval to heart-shaped leaves and many flower heads. These flowers have a brown center disk often surrounded by a double row of bright yellow ray florets, which turn to face the sun as it moves across the sky. Sunflower is one of the few food staples originating in North America. The Indians used the seeds for food and oil, the flowers for dye, the stems for a rough cloth, and the leaves for horse fodder.

## SUNFLOWER, SAWTOOTH - *Helianthus grosseserratus*

| July - Oct. | Grows to 16 feet. |
|---|---|

This tall sunflower has many branches, each one with a typical sunflower head of yellow ray florets around a yellow center disk. These blossoms are up to 3 inches across, slightly smaller than the common Sunflower. The leaves are lance shaped and coarsely toothed with the undersurface being white and downy.

## GOLDENROD - *Solidago sp.*

| Aug. - Nov. | Grows from 2 - 7 feet. |
|---|---|

There are over 60 species of this member of the sunflower family. The clusters of tiny yellow flowers grow on arching branches. Goldenrod is often wrongly blamed for hay fever, but its pollen is sticky not wind borne. The true culprit is usually ragweed pollen. Goldenrod is a perennial, which spreads to form large clumps. In former times it was occasionally used to treat wounds.

ShR
10/0

## DAY LILY - *Hemerocallis fulva*

| May - Aug. | Grows from 2-4 feet. |
|---|---|

The Day Lily's bright orange flowers with yellow centers are made up of 3 sepals and 3 petals. They are about 3 1/2 inches across and each blossom lasts one day. The orange varieties have no scent. They have long basal straplike leaves. Day Lilies spread by root division since the flowers are sterile. The flowers are rich in protein and are eaten in China.

SKR
6/98          Day lily

## TRUMPETVINE (TRUMPET CREEPER) - *Campsis radicans*

| May - Aug. | Vine |
|---|---|

Trumpetvine has aerial rootlets that turn woody allowing it to become quite tall as it climbs up a support. The red to orange trumpet shaped flowers are 2-2 1/2 inches long and form long hanging seedpods. The leaves are compound with 6-8 opposite and one terminal leaflet. They are coarse toothed and pointed. The flowers attract hummingbirds as well as insects.

SKR 8/05

## CARDINAL FLOWER - *Lobelia cardinalis*

| July-Sept. | Grows from 2-5 feet. |
|---|---|

The stalks of the Cardinal Flower are at first unbranched, but later have flowering side branches. Each blossom has 2 partial upper lips and a 3 divided lower lip with protruding stamens. The brilliant red color matches that worn by the cardinals of the Roman Church. These plants are usually found along the edges of ditches and streams, preferring low wet areas. They are becoming scarce. This is a native flower of the Lobelia family, unusual because most lobelias are blue in color.

## FLEABANE, PHILIDELPHIA - *Erigeron philadelphicus*

| April - June. | Grows from 1-3 feet. |
|---|---|

The stems are branched toward the top and have hairy, usually toothed, clasping leaves. The buds are drooping, but the flowers are erect. Each flower has a yellow center surrounded by 150 - 200 pink rays, the most of any Erigeron. The native Americans had many uses for this plant from treating wounds to head colds.

Philadelphia

SKR
5/03

## BEARD TONGUE - *Penstemon hirsutus*

| May - June. | Grows 1 - 3 feet. |
|---|---|

Beard Tongue has a tall straight stem with small, tubular, white or pale pink flowers in clusters. Penstemon is Greek for 5 stamens. The 5th one protrudes and is covered with pale hairs or bearded. Only certain insects are able to push through this to get to the nectar. This is a native perennial with a strong fragrance.

SKR
6/03

## ROSE, PASTURE - *Rosa Arkansana*

| May - June | Grows from 1 - 3 feet. |
| --- | --- |

Each Rose flower has five heart shaped petals and the leaves usually have 7 leaflets growing on prickly stems. The color ranges from pale to deep pink. Each blossom lasts only one day, spreading its light perfume in the sunshine. The rose is known throughout the world. In fact the same word is used in English, French, German, Danish, and Norwegian. The rose is the national flower of England, while the wild rose is the state flower of three states.

## BERGAMOT, WILD (BEE BALM) -*Monarda fistulosa*

| May - Aug. | Grows to 3 feet. |
|---|---|

Wild Bergamot is a native perennial. The blossoms consist of rose-purple floral tubes 1 1/2 inches long in terminal clusters. They are attractive to butterflies and humming birds. The stem is square sided while the leaves are velvety and opposite. It got its name because it smells like the fragrant Bergamot Orange, a citrus plant with a minty smell. The Indians used it to scent their bear grease.

Wild Bergamot

7/9?
SKR

## CULVER'S ROOT - *Veronicastrum virginicum*

| June - Sept. | Grows from 2-7 feet. |
|---|---|

The leaves of Culver's Root are smooth and grow in whorls. The white or pale pink tubular flowers are tightly spaced on spikes. They have protruding pale-colored pistils. This perennial had medicinal uses and was named for Dr. Coulvert an American of the late 17th century. Some Indians used Culver's Root in purification ceremonies.

| MILKWEED - *Asclepias syriaca* | |
|---|---|
| May - Aug. | Grows to 5 feet. |

The stems of the milkweed plant are thick and exude a sticky, white sap that discourages insects. The leaves are broad ovals on distinct stems. Monarch butterflies lay their eggs on these leaves. The small pink to lilac flowers grow in a spherical cluster. The early spring shoots may be eaten like asparagus. In WWII children collected the seedpods to use in filling life jackets.

## CLOVER, RED - *Trifolium pratense*

| May-Sept. | Grows from 1-3 feet. |
|-----------|----------------------|

Red Clover is common in all grassy places and grows along most roadsides throughout Illinois. The magenta flowers grow in round heads. There are 3 oval leaflets usually marked with a white V. The occasional 4-leaved mutation is considered good luck. Bees love Red Clover and make a flavorful honey from its nectar. All clovers have long been cultivated by man for fodder and to improve the soil.

SKR 6/04

## BOUNCING BET (SOAPWORT) - *Saponaria officinalis*

| June - Oct. | Grows to 2 feet. |
|---|---|

The pale pink flowers of Bouncing Bet grow in open groups. Each flower has five notched petals coming from a long tube. They are pleasantly fragrant. The leaves are opposite, slightly wavy and have three main veins. This plant is a native of Europe and was brought to America by the colonists. The early pioneers used suds from pounding the roots for washing clothes. Bouncing Bet is an old nickname for a washerwoman.

## SMARTWEED - *Polygonum amphibian*

| June - Oct. | Grows to 3 feet. |
|---|---|

Smartweed grows in dense colonies both in water and on land. The stems are smooth and branched with swollen nodes hence the name polygonum meaning many knees. The flowers are in racemes of tiny pink blossoms often arching downward. The fruit provides food for wildlife.

SKR 10/05

## GERMANDER, AMERICAN - *Teucrium canadense*

| July - Aug. | Grows from 1 - 3 feet. |
|---|---|

Germander is a member of the mint family and has the typical square stem. The blossoms grow in terminal spikes on top of rarely branched stems. The small lavender - pink petals form a large lower lip, which fades to tan as the flower matures. The Latin name comes from Teicer, the first king of Troy, who may have used a European variety as a medicine.

SKR
%.04

## HENBIT (DEADNETTLE) - *Lamium amplexicaule*

| Febuary - Nov. | Grows to 10 inches. |
|---|---|

Henbit is a winter annual member of the mint family. It is a native of Europe and Asia. The lower leaves are stalked, while the upper leaves clasp the square stem. The bright rose-colored tubular flowers grow in whorls in the axils of the upper scalloped leaves. It is one of the earliest flowers to be noticed blooming along side the roads and in yards. The Latin name means throat referring to the shape of the flower.

## VIOLET, BLUE - *Viola sororia*

| March - June. | Grow to 6 inches tall. |
|---|---|

Violet leaves are heart-shaped, each one on its own stem. The flowers have five blue or purple petals, but because of cross breeding there are infinite variations in colors. Picking does not seem to bother violets since they spread by extending the root stock as well as by seeds which are often dispersed by ants. Four states have the violet as their state flower: Illinois, New Jersey, Rhode Island, and Wisconsin. The blossoms are sometimes candied to garnish special desserts.

Blue
Violet

SKR
5/03

## SPIDERWORT - *Tradescantia ohiensis*

| May - June. | Grows to 3 feet. |
| --- | --- |

These bright blue flowers have 3 petals in a triangular pattern. The dark blue stamens are bearded and fluffy. The blossom of the morning melts to a drop of purple in the hot sun by afternoon. The buds hang down on reddish stems, bend up to bloom, then back down to form seeds. The leaves are long, narrow, and folded lengthwise. It was named after John Tradescant, King Charles's gardener, who once planted a garden in which you could tell time by which flowers were blooming.

## DAME'S ROCKET - *Hesperis matronalis*

| May - June. | Grows from 2 - 4 feet. |
|---|---|

This member of the mustard family is a perennial or biennial. On the upright branches are loosely grouped, purple flowers each with 4 petals in the shape of a cross. The long seedpods germinate easily allowing the plant to create dense stands which crowd out native species. Dame's Rocket seeds are often included in wildflower seed mixes sold commercially, although it is actually an escaped ornamental. The flowers have very little scent during daylight hours, but release a sweet, violet-like scent at night.

SKR 5/03

## BLUE FLAG - *Iris shrevei*

| May - July. | Grows from 2-3 feet. |
| --- | --- |

These blue flowers consist of 3 sepals called falls and 3 upright petals called standards. Veins on the falls lead bees deep into the nectar and pollen. The leaves are mostly basal and strap like. Iris grows in wet meadows and ditches. Iris was the goddess of the rainbow so the many colors of Iris blossoms led to the name. Louis VII of France used the Iris in his coat of arms. The design is known as the fleur-de-lys.

## IRONWEED - *Vernonia baldwini*

| May - Sept. | Grows to 4 feet. |
|---|---|

Ironweed is a perennial with stiff upright branches. At the top of these branches are clusters of numerous flower heads. Each flower is about 1/2 inch across with many rose-purple floret rays. The leaves are alternate, hairy, and pointed at both ends with short stems. The scientific name comes from William Vernon and William Baldwin who were botanists in the 1600's and 1700's.

## CHICORY - *Cichorium intybus*

| May - Oct. | Grows to 3 feet. |
| --- | --- |

Chicory will continue to bloom inches from the ground after being mowed down. It has a rosette of basal leaves similar to the Dandelion but has very few leaves on the upper branches. Despite the heat and passing cars, Chicory borders the highways throughout the state. The early settlers roasted the roots for a coffee-like drink. In fact the word chicory comes from the Arabic word for coffee. Early prospectors thought it brought good luck on trips and would sometimes carry a root in their pocket.

## WILD FOUR O'CLOCK - *Mirabilis nyctaginea*

| May - Aug. | Grows from 1 - 3 feet. |
|---|---|

Wild Four O'Clocks are much smaller than the ornamental garden variety Four O'Clocks. The bell-shaped lavender blossoms open in the early morning and close by mid-afternoon. They have no real petals. Instead, it is the sepals which are colored. They have opposite heart shaped leaves and jointed stems, which usually branch above each pair of leaves. It is a native species.

Wild Four O'clocks

SKR
6/96

## PETUNIA, WILD - *Ruellia strepens*

| May - Oct. | Grows from 6 inches to 2 feet. |
|---|---|

Wild Petunia has opposite oval leaves and lavender tubular flowers which develop one or two in leaf axils near the middle of the stems. The stems and leaves are slightly hairy. The five-lobed blossoms are gently wrinkled and each blossom lasts for only one day. This native plant is not really a member of the Petunia family.

## DAYFLOWER - *Commelina communis*

| June - Aug. | Grows 1-2 feet. |
|---|---|

The scientific name of the Dayflower was given by
Linnaeus in honor of the Commelin brothers. The 2 bright
blue petals represent the 2 who were respected scientists,
while the small white petal stood for the 3rd brother who
died young. It is a member of the Spiderwort family. The
flowers emerge one at a time from a boat like sheath. The
long, narrow, lance-shaped leaves clasp the stem.

## CONEFLOWER, PURPLE - *Echinacea purpurea*

| June - Oct. | Grows to 4 feet. |
|---|---|

There are 9 species in the Echinacea genus, and all are native to North America. Purple Coneflower has a stiff hairy stem topped by a single large blossom. The purple pink rays droop from the bristly orange head. It is sometimes used as an herbal supplement thought to boost the immune system. Echinacea is the Greek word for hedgehog.

## THISTLE, BULL - *Cirsium vulgare*

| June - Sept. | Grows to 7 feet. |
|---|---|

Bull thistle has very prickly leaves and the stems are winged with wavy prickly tissue. The spines on the base grow right up to the flower head. The globe shaped flower consists of many thin tubes of lavender or rose. It is common in pastures and waste places. The seeds are preferred by Goldfinches, who also use the fluff to line their nests.

| THISTLE, CANADA - *Cirsium arvense* | |
|---|---|
| June - Oct. | Grows from 1 - 4 feet. |

This many branched plant has numerous small purple flower heads about 1/2 inch across. It is difficult to eradicate because of creeping underground stems which help it form into dense patches. That is why it is sometimes called Creeping Thistle. It is not a native of Canada, rather it comes from Europe and Asia. It is classified as a noxious weed.

## THISTLE, NODDING (MUSK THISTLE) - *Carduus nutans*

| June - Oct. | Grows to 6 feet. |
|---|---|

The flower heads of Nodding Thistle are up to 2 1/2 inches across. The rose purple blossoms are surrounded by recurved bracts. The mature heads nod in the breeze. The basal rosette forms the first year and stays green all winter. The upright stem appears the second year with smaller spiny leaves. Unchecked it easily out competes smaller native plants.

| MORNING GLORY - *Ipomoea convolulsus* ||
|---|---|
| July - Oct. | Vine. |

This native of tropical America has twining vines with ivy shaped leaves. It seems undisturbed by cinders, smoke, or grime, as it will grow almost anywhere. Other members of the morning glory family may have heart-shaped or arrow shaped leaves. The pink, blue or purple blossoms open every dawn and usually close by noon.

SKR 8/05

# Index

# Bibliography

*The following books were used as resources for this work.*

Courtenay, Booth and James H. Zimmerman. *"Wildflowers and Weeds"* New York: Van Nostrand Reinhold CO., 1972.

Denison, Edgar. *"Missouri Wildflowers"* Fifth Edition. Jefferson City, MO.: Missouri Dept. of Conservation, 1998.

Mehlenbrock, Robert H. *"Wildflowers of Fields, Roadsides, and Open Habitats of Illinois."* Springfield, IL. Dept. of Conservation Division of Forest Resources and Natural Hertitage.

Peterson, Roger Tory and Margaret McKenny. *"A Field Guide to Wildflowers , Northeastern and North-central North America."* Boston: Houghton Mifflin Co., 1968.

Peterson, Roger Tory. *"Peterson First Guide to Wildflowers of Northeastern and North-central North America."* Boston, New York:Houghton Mifflin Co., 1986.

Spellenberg, Richard. *"National Audubon Society Pocket Guide: Familiar Flowers of North America, Eastern Region."* New York: Alfred A. Knopf, Inc., 1986.

Stubbendieck, James and Geir Y. Friisoe and Margaret R. Bolick. *"Weeds of Nebraska and the Great Plains."* Lincoln, Nebraska: Nebraska Dept. of Agriculture, 1995.

Voigt, John W. and Robert H. Mohlenbrock. *"Prairie Plants of Illinois."* Springfield, IL.: Illinois Dept. of Conservation, (45263-10M-3-85).

Voss, John and Virginia S. Eifert. *"Illinois Wild Flowers."* Springfield, IL.: Illinois State Museum, 1951.

Wax, Loyd M. and Richard Fawcett and Duane Isely. *"Weeds of the North Central States."* Urbana, IL.: University of Illinois at Urbana-Champaign. College of Agriculture, 1981.

# Map Key

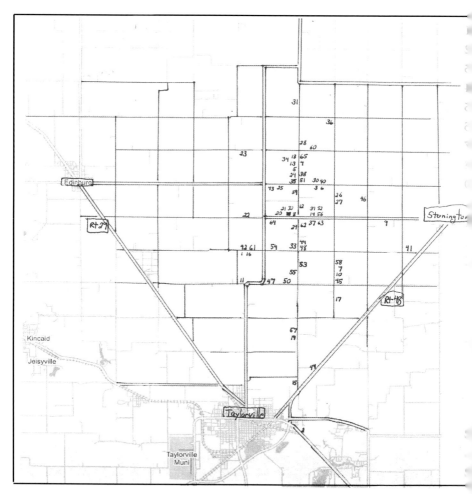

*Although some wildflowers are edible, there are many poisonous species which*

1. Aster, Frost
2. Beard Tongue
3. Bergamot, Wild
4. Bird's Foot Trefoil
5. Blackberry
6. Black-eyed Susan
7. Blue Flag
8. Bouncing Bet
9. Butter and Eggs
10. Campion, White
11. Cardinal Flower
12. Chicory
13. Cinquefoil, Rough-fruited
14. Clover, Red
15. Compass Plant
16. Coneflower, Purple
17. Groundsel, Cress-leaf
18. Culver's Root
19. Dame's Rocket
20. Dandelion
21. Dayflower
22. Day Lily

23. Dock, Prairie
24. Dogbane
25. Evening Primrose
26. Fleabane, Daisy
27. Fleabane, Philadelphia
28. Flower of an Hour
29. Wild Four O'clock
30. Germander, American
31. Goldenrod
32. Ground Ivy
33. Henbit
34. Ironweed
35. Milkweed
36. Morning Glory
37. Mullein, Moth
38. Mullein, Great
39. Nettle, Horse
40. Onion, Wild
41. Parsley, Hedge
42. Parsnip, Wild
43. Partridge Pea
44. Pennycress

45. Petunia, Wild
46. Pokeweed
47. Poison Hemlock
48. Queen Anne's Lace
49. Rose, Wild Pasture
50. Yellow Salsify
51. Saint John's Wort
52. Smartweed
53. Sowthistle, Spiny
54. Spiderwort
55. Strawberry, Wild
56. Sunflower, Common
57. Sunflower, Sawtooth
58. Teasel
59. Thistle, Bull
60. Thistle, Canada
61. Thistle, Nodding
62. Trumpet Vine
63. Violet, Blue
64. Yarrow, Milfoil
65. Yellow Rocket

ifficult to distinguish. *Do not eat any plant you find growing wild.*

# Field Notes

Dale
We are goo